D1221256

FORENSIC Investigations

NATURE TELLS

Looking at Bugs, Plants, and the Environment

Leela Burnscott

Smart Apple Media

Smart Apple Media
P.O. Box 3263
Mankato, MN 56002

First published in 2009 by
MACMILLAN EDUCATION AUSTRALIA PTY LTD
15–19 Claremont Street, South Yarra 3141

Visit our website at www.macmillan.com.au or go directly to www.macmillanlibrary.com.au

Associated companies and representatives throughout the world.

Copyright © Leela Burnscott 2009

Library of Congress Cataloging-in-Publication Data

Burnscott, Leela.
    Nature tells: looking at bugs, plants and the environment / Leela Burnscott.
       p. cm. -- (Forensic investigations)
    Includes index.
    ISBN 978-1-59920-462-8 (hardcover)
    1. Forensic sciences—Juvenile literature. 2. Evidence, Criminal—Juvenile literature. 3. Criminal investigation—Juvenile literature.
    4. Crime scene searches—Juvenile literature. I. Title.
    HV8073.8.B869 2010
    363.25'62—dc22

                                                                    2009003450

Edited by Georgina Garner
Text and cover design by Cristina Neri, Canary Graphic Design
Page layout by Raul Diche
Photo research by Sarah Johnson
Illustrations by Alan Laver, Shelly Communications

Printed in the United States

Acknowledgments
The author and the publisher are grateful to the following for permission to reproduce copyright material:

Front cover photograph: Forensic scientist sampling flies found on a corpse, © Philippe Psaila/Science Photo Library/Photolibrary

Background images used throughout pages: fingerprint courtesy of iStockphoto/James Steidl; tweezers courtesy of iStockphoto/Mitar Holod; forensic investigation kit courtesy of iStockphoto/Brandon Alms.

Images courtesy of: © Bettmann/Corbis, 28; Clemson University – USDA Cooperative Extension Slide Series, United States, 16; Richard Gosling/Fairfax Photos, 27; Getty Images/Dan Trevan/AFP, 4; Getty Images/Photo by Hulton Archive, 29; Getty Images/Reza Estakhrian, 26; iStockphoto, 12, 30 (middle left and middle right); iStockphoto/Achim Prill, 8; iStockphoto/Arjan de Jager, 25 (bottom); iStockphoto/Dan Roundhill, 18; iStockphoto/Josh Hodge, 25 (top); iStockphoto/Mikhail Olykaynen, 23; iStockphoto/Pamela Moore, 30 (top left); iStockphoto/Sebastien Cote, 25 (second); iStockphoto/Slobo Mitic, 6; iStockphoto/Sondra Paulson, 22 (top); iStockphoto/Svetlana Prikhodko, 5; iStockphoto/Tatjana Brila, 22 (third); © School of Biological Sciences, University of Sydney, 10; Adam Hart-Davis/Science Photo Library/Photolibrary, 25 (third); Peter Menzel/Science Photo Library/Photolibrary, 20; Philippe Psaila/Science Photo Library/Photolibrary, 30 (top right); Steve Gschmeissner/Science Photo Library/Photolibrary, 21; Susumu Nishinaga/Science Photo Library/Photolibrary, 22 (second and bottom); Shutterstock/Alistair Scott, 17; Shutterstock/Frances A. Miller, 19; Shutterstock/Kevin Phillips, 13; Shutterstock/Marek Pawluczuk, 7; Shutterstock/Mitchell Brothers 21st Century Film Group, 24; Shutterstock/Simon Krzic, 15; Shutterstock/Thomas Mounsey, 14; Image copyright © Victorian Institute of Forensic Medicine, 30 (bottom).

While every care has been taken to trace and acknowledge copyright, the publisher tenders their apologies for any accidental infringement where copyright has proved untraceable. Where the attempt has been unsuccessful, the publisher welcomes information that would redress the situation.

Contents

GLOSSARY WORDS

When a word is printed in **bold**, you can look up its meaning in the Glossary on page 31.

Science in the Court!

Forensic science is the use of scientific knowledge and techniques within the legal system, particularly in the investigation of crime. Forensic science can:

- determine if an **incident** resulted from an accident, natural causes, or a criminal act
- identify those involved in the incident
- identify and find those people responsible for the incident
- make sure that the innocent are not wrongly convicted

The term "forensic science" is quite misleading because it suggests only one type of science is involved. This is certainly not the case. Forensic investigations can involve virtually every field of science and technology, from electronics to psychology.

Forensic investigations require the skills of specially trained police, scientists, doctors, engineers, and other professionals. These investigators examine all types of evidence, from bloodstains to weapons and from bugs to computers. The greater the pool of evidence against an accused person, the greater the chance of a conviction.

A forensic expert presents crime scene photographs during a trial.

Nature Tells

To most people, nature is a beautiful thing and something to be enjoyed. To a forensic investigator, nature is one of the most reliable and dedicated crime-fighters. Bugs, plants, and the environment can reveal many aspects of a case, such as:

- who committed a crime or caused an accident
- the time of death or injury
- where a victim is being held or is buried
- the movements of a victim, suspect, or vehicle

The environment, animals, and plants all have characteristics that forensic scientists, such as chemists, **botanists**, and **entomologists**, can analyze to reveal their tales.

Leaf litter and insects such as ants can be useful forensic tools.

Soil

Soil is nature's rubbish dump. It is a mix of minerals and other leftovers from worn-away rocks, bushfires, dead plants, fallen leaves, animal feeds, animal waste, and dead animals.

Soil is often used as a rubbish dump by humans, too. Chemicals, paints, paper, food scraps, and tyres are just some of the things people throw into the ground.

To a forensic investigator, soil is an endless source of treasures that can help solve crimes. The **composition** of soil can vary widely from place to place, making it an ideal forensic tracking tool. In this book, soil includes sand, mud, dirt, rocks, and all types of earth.

DID YOU KNOW?

Rocks are formed over millions of years from compressed soil and minerals. Wind and water cause the rocks to **erode**. The eroded material returns to the soil, where it may eventually form new rocks.

The erosion channels in this soil were produced by years of water running over the land into the river.

Soil Samples

Soil is a forensic investigator's best friend. It is easily picked up by people and objects, including during crimes, without anyone noticing. Forensic investigators, however, notice soil and collect it from under fingernails, clothing, the **tread** of shoes and tires, and from objects such as cars, shovels, and weapons.

Soil examiners are also called upon to help find the cause of soil pollution. Sometimes, pollution may be the result of an accident or **negligence**, such as an oil spill at sea, a leaky underground factory pipe, or a truck that overturns and spills its chemical cargo. Other times, pollutants are deliberately and illegally dumped. The culprits need to be tracked down and taken to court.

Soil trapped in the tread of a tire can be recovered for forensic examination.

Soil Evidence

Soil evidence can help forensic investigators determine if a body has been moved, or link a vehicle, weapon, or person to a crime scene or body dumpsite.

Different types of soils have different compositions. This often allows investigators to pinpoint the area the soil sample came from, such as a vegetable garden, a dry wasteland, or an industrial area.

Forensic chemists analyze:

- the mineral composition of the soil
- the plant or **organic** materials that are present
- if there are any chemical **contaminants**
- the physical characteristics of the soil, such as colour, texture, and absorbency

CASE NOTE

In cases of environmental pollution, pollutants are extracted from the soil and analyzed. These are then matched to samples taken from possible pollution sources to identify the guilty party.

Chemical contaminants can pollute soil and the environment.

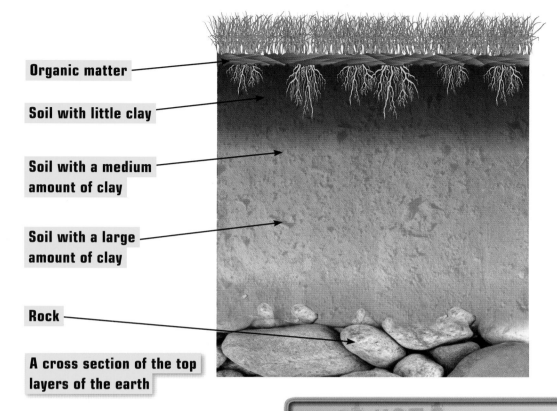

Organic matter

Soil with little clay

Soil with a medium amount of clay

Soil with a large amount of clay

Rock

A cross section of the top layers of the earth

Soil Texture and Absorbency

The texture of soil depends mainly on the amount of clay, sand, and **silt** present. This also controls how much water soil can absorb or hold.

Soil with little clay content is found in the top layers of earth. It has a very fine texture, does not clump together, and absorbs very little water. This allows water to flow freely through it. Soil with a medium amount of clay is thicker, more absorbent, and clumpier.

Soil with a lot of clay is generally found deep under the surface. These soils have very little organic matter in them. They absorb much more water than other soil types and form thick, damp, yellow–brown clumps that can be easily shaped.

CASE NOTE

When clay soil gets wet, it sticks firmly to objects. When it dries, it turns rock-hard and is very difficult to remove. Forensic investigators can use this to their advantage. They can link a soil-encrusted shovel to the place where something or someone was buried.

Insects

Insects may seem like insignificant little creatures, but in the world of forensic science they are crime-fighting giants. Entomology is the study of insects and other arthropods, such as spiders. Forensic entomology covers three broad fields, called stored products, urban, and medico-legal entomology.

Insect Evidence

Forensic entomologists look for insects in many places, such as:

- within the flesh of a corpse or injured person
- flying around a victim
- on a victim's or suspect's clothing
- in the hair of a victim or suspect
- on or in a car used to transport a victim
- in food samples
- in buildings and wood products
- on animals

The most common insects that forensic entomologists work with are blowflies, beetles, and cockroaches. Cockroaches and some beetles have strong mouthparts, called mandibles, which can damage human skin. Cockroaches have also been known to eat human hair, removing valuable evidence from a crime scene.

A cockroach uses its strong mandible to break down materials, such as food scraps, human skin, and even wood.

Collecting Insects

Entomologists find, collect, and examine:

- live insects or dead insects
- whole insects or parts of insects
- eggs, young forms, and adult forms of insects
- larval casts or skins from when young insects moult
- pupal cases, such as cocoons

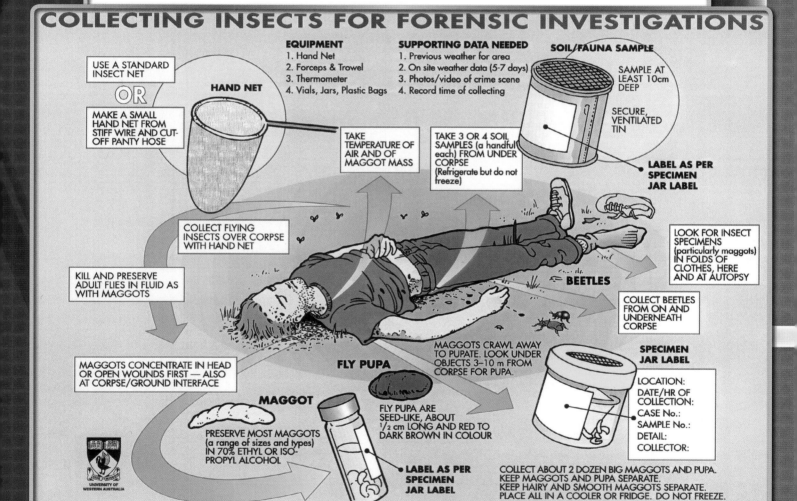

COLLECTING INSECTS FOR FORENSIC INVESTIGATIONS

USE A STANDARD INSECT NET

OR

MAKE A SMALL HAND NET FROM STIFF WIRE AND CUT-OFF PANTY HOSE

HAND NET

EQUIPMENT
1. Hand Net
2. Forceps & Trowel
3. Thermometer
4. Vials, Jars, Plastic Bags

SUPPORTING DATA NEEDED
1. Previous weather for area
2. On site weather data (5-7 days)
3. Photos/video of crime scene
4. Record time of collecting

SOIL/FAUNA SAMPLE

SAMPLE AT LEAST 10cm DEEP

SECURE, VENTILATED TIN

TAKE TEMPERATURE OF AIR AND OF MAGGOT MASS

TAKE 3 OR 4 SOIL SAMPLES (a handful each) FROM UNDER CORPSE (Refrigerate but do not freeze)

LABEL AS PER SPECIMEN JAR LABEL

COLLECT FLYING INSECTS OVER CORPSE WITH HAND NET

LOOK FOR INSECT SPECIMENS (particularly maggots) IN FOLDS OF CLOTHES, HERE AND AT AUTOPSY

KILL AND PRESERVE ADULT FLIES IN FLUID AS WITH MAGGOTS

BEETLES

COLLECT BEETLES FROM ON AND UNDERNEATH CORPSE

MAGGOTS CONCENTRATE IN HEAD OR OPEN WOUNDS FIRST — ALSO AT CORPSE/GROUND INTERFACE

FLY PUPA

MAGGOTS CRAWL AWAY TO PUPATE. LOOK UNDER OBJECTS 3–10 m FROM CORPSE FOR PUPA.

SPECIMEN JAR LABEL

MAGGOT

FLY PUPA ARE SEED-LIKE, ABOUT ½ cm LONG AND RED TO DARK BROWN IN COLOUR

PRESERVE MOST MAGGOTS (a range of sizes and types) IN 70% ETHYL OR ISO-PROPYL ALCOHOL

LOCATION:
DATE/HR OF COLLECTION:
CASE No.:
SAMPLE No.:
DETAIL:
COLLECTOR:

UNIVERSITY OF WESTERN AUSTRALIA

LABEL AS PER SPECIMEN JAR LABEL

COLLECT ABOUT 2 DOZEN BIG MAGGOTS AND PUPA. KEEP MAGGOTS AND PUPA SEPARATE. KEEP HAIRY AND SMOOTH MAGGOTS SEPARATE. PLACE ALL IN A COOLER OR FRIDGE. DO NOT FREEZE.

An entomologist collects all the different forms of insects at a crime scene.

An insect infestation of a bag of rice may require investigation by a forensic entomologist.

Stored Products Entomology

This field deals with investigating insect contamination of food products, such as bread or take-away foods. Contamination is sometimes accidental. Sometimes, it is the result of unhygienic and negligent work practices, or even deliberate contamination.

If the contamination is accidental, the seller or producer is unlikely to face criminal charges. They would be asked to make changes to prevent any contamination from happening again. They may be **sued** by the person who bought the product.

When the contamination is due to poor work practices, the business could be shut down and the owners fined or even charged with a crime. Deliberate contamination is a criminal offence. It is often done to make a false **compensation** claim, to damage the reputation of the food producer or seller, or to blackmail them.

Urban Entomology

Urban entomologists work on cases that involve insect **infestations** in houses, farms, hospitals, **mortuaries**, and any other human environment.

Cases may involve termite-infested or termite-damaged houses. An agent or a property owner could be sued by a new buyer if they sell a house without mentioning that it is or was once infested by termites.

A farmer or homeowner could sue their neighbor over an insect infestation on their property or in their livestock, if it is proven that the infestation was caused by the neighbor's neglect of their farm. Someone who uses their yard as a rubbish dump could develop a cockroach problem, which could spread to other yards.

Hospitals can be charged with medical neglect if insects are regularly found in the hospital or in patients' wounds. Maggot-infested corpses in a mortuary would be another case of neglect.

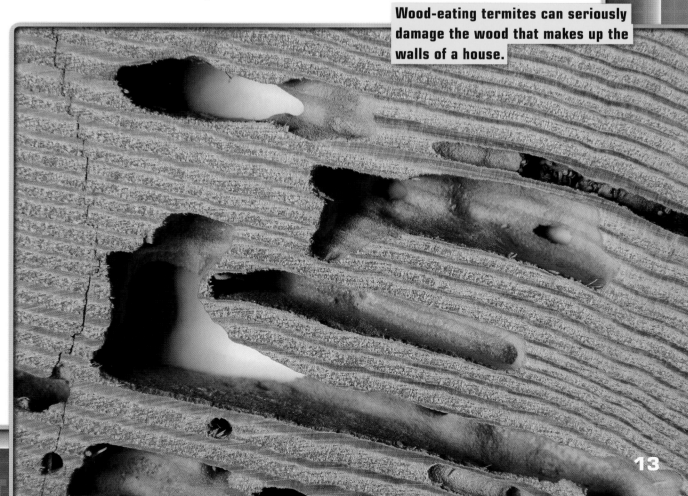

Wood-eating termites can seriously damage the wood that makes up the walls of a house.

Medico-Legal Entomology

Medico-legal entomology involves looking at how insects could cause an incident, alter the evidence, or provide evidence. Entomologists can be called in to investigate:

- insect damage to a body
- unusual bloodstain patterns
- unexplained deaths or accidents
- approximate time of death
- the location of a crime scene or corpse
- the presence of poisons in a corpse

Damage and Bloodstains

When insects chew on skin and flesh, they produce marks that can be misinterpreted as signs of abuse or mistreatment. Insect bite marks may look like "gravel rash," wrongly suggesting that a body was dragged along the ground. Forensic entomologists may be asked to examine damage to a body to determine if insects could have caused the damage.

Insects can also lead to the misinterpretation of bloodstains. When an insect walks through or lands on wet blood, its feet become bloody. Wherever it walks or lands next, small spots of blood are left behind. Forensic entomologists can help with unexplained blood spots on a wall, ceiling, or unrelated area.

DID YOU KNOW?

"Medico-legal" means relating to both medicine and law.

Maggots feed on animal tissue and food products.

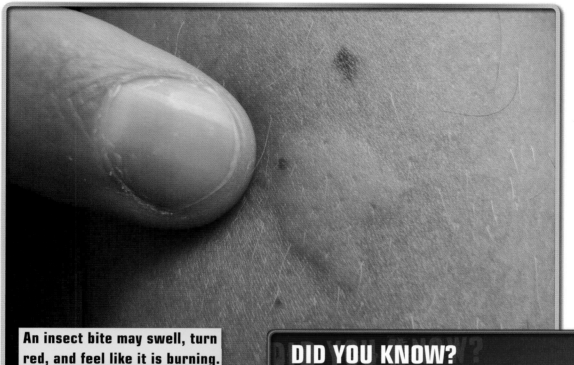

An insect bite may swell, turn red, and feel like it is burning.

Unexplained Deaths

When a perfectly healthy person drops dead for no apparent reason, a lethal insect bite or poisoning are two possibilities that are investigated. Insects can have two roles in these unexplained deaths. They could be the cause of death or they could help to reveal the cause.

Some spider venoms are highly poisonous and can kill within hours, while others are only lethal if a victim is allergic to the venom. Bee and wasp stings are usually only fatal if the person is allergic to them.

If a person has been poisoned but the body is badly decomposed and there is no hair or tissue left to test, all is not lost. The maggots that fed on the body take up the poison. Entomologists can extract and analyze these poisons from the maggots or their larval casts.

Time and Location of Death

An approximate time of death can be found by looking at the types of insects found on a corpse. Different types of insects settle on a corpse at different times as it decomposes.

Type of Insect on Corpse	Age of Corpse
Blowflies	0–3 months
Dermestid beetles	3–6 months
Various flies and beetles	4–8 months
Mites	6–12 months
Dermestid beetles	1–3 years
Beetles	3 or more years

Determining what stage in their life cycle the insects are in gives even more information about the time of death. The time spent by an insect in each of its growth phases is fixed. Temperature, however, can cause some variation in these times. This is why entomologists must always take into account the temperature at the scene and the temperature of the body.

The place a person was killed or first buried can also be discovered by looking at the insects on the body. This is because certain insects are found only in certain areas.

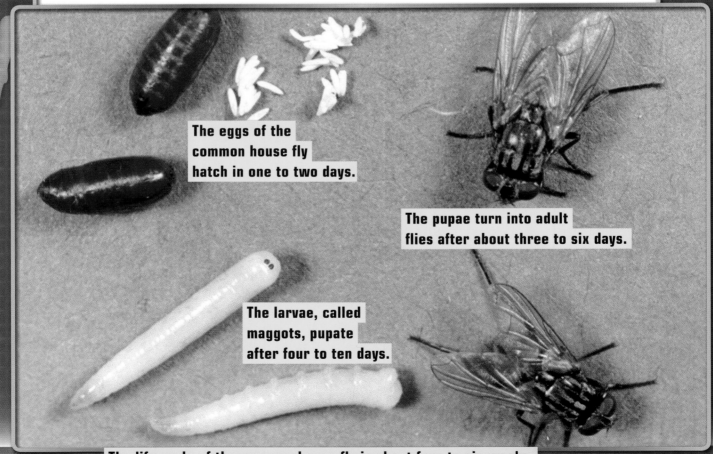

The eggs of the common house fly hatch in one to two days.

The pupae turn into adult flies after about three to six days.

The larvae, called maggots, pupate after four to ten days.

The life cycle of the common house fly is about four to six weeks.

Insects and Accidents

Believe it or not, insects are responsible for a small number of accidents each year. The most common accidents are car crashes in which a driver drives off the road or into another vehicle. These accidents happen when drivers lose control of their cars when they are stung or bitten by a bee, spider, or insect, or when they become distracted by a spider on their windscreen or by a bee buzzing around their face.

It is not just drivers that can have insect-related accidents. People do all sorts of dangerous things when confronted by insects. They might run into the path of a car or fall off a balcony while trying to escape from a wasp, or because of the pain of an insect bite.

A man collects a swarm of bees in a collecting box, taking care not to be stung.

DID YOU KNOW?

Insects have been linked to some airplane crashes. They may have blocked fuel lines, causing engine failure, or affected essential instruments.

Animals

Animals often only play a small role in solving a forensic investigation, but they can play a large role in hampering or misleading an investigation. This is why zoologists, who study the physical, biological, and behavioral aspects of animals, are important forensic investigators.

Contaminating a Crime Scene

Animals can be an investigator's worst nightmare. They can contaminate or destroy a crime scene by:

- removing objects such as clothing, weapons, or body parts from the crime scene
- disturbing the crime scene by knocking over objects or accidentally moving them around
- contaminating the crime scene by leaving behind hairs, blood, or saliva, or by bringing in soil, plant matter, and other objects
- smudging or spreading bloodstains
- biting or scratching evidence or a victim, leading investigators to wrongly believe that the victim was physically abused

Animals, such as bears, may disturb a crime scene by scattering objects as they search for food.

A police dog is used to sniff out drugs in a car.

Crime-Fighting

Animals can also be an investigator's best friend. Dogs are excellent at sniffing out dumped or buried bodies. In fact, sometimes it is someone's pet dog on its daily walk that makes the discovery that sets off a forensic investigation. Police forces around the world now train dogs specifically to sniff out flesh, drugs, gunpowder, or bombs to help in the fight against crime.

Animal hair, fur, and feathers are also useful forensic evidence. Finding hair or feathers from a suspect's pet on a victim, on a weapon, in a "get-away" car, or at a crime scene can link a suspect to a crime.

Finding traces of animals on a recently discovered body can occasionally help determine the time and place of death. This is because, like insects, some animals only live in certain places and only venture out at certain times of the day or night.

Plants

Plants are often vital pieces of forensic evidence. Botany, which is the study of plants, has been used as a forensic science since the early 1900s, and it is widely accepted by courts.

Forensic botanists may:

- examine any traces of plant material found in soil at a crime scene or on clothing, weapons, tools, or other objects involved in a crime
- analyze wooden tools or weapons used in a crime
- identify plants growing in the wild or illegally on a property

The results of these investigations could determine:

- the season and location in which a crime took place
- if a body was moved from a murder site
- how long a body has been buried
- if plant-based poisons or **narcotics** are involved or have been produced

They can also link a suspect, weapon, tool, or vehicle to a crime or crime scene.

These forensic investigators search for evidence among leaf litter.

Plant Evidence

Plant evidence can be microscopic or **macroscopic**. Microscopic plant material may be pollen, spores, **trichomes**, cells and cell structure, and DNA. Macroscopic plant material may be wood, charcoal, seeds, fruits, leaves, twigs, or flowers.

Plant material can be picked up by almost anything and, like soil, it often goes unnoticed by a culprit. Forensic experts can recover plant evidence from almost everywhere. It can even be recovered from the stomach contents of a deceased person.

The biggest problem in forensic botany is that the macroscopic features of plant material can look very similar. Experienced forensic botanists, however, use microscopic characteristics to identify plant species.

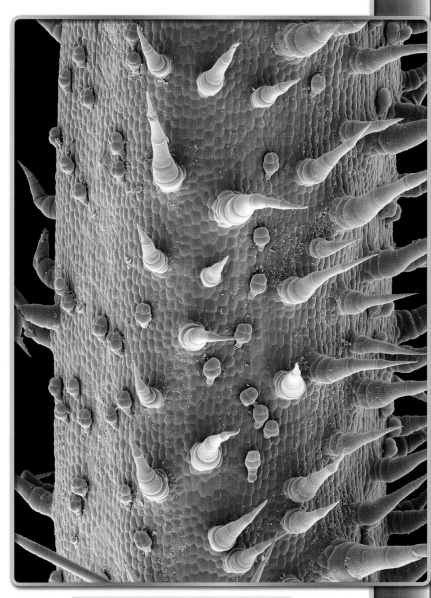

The hair and trichomes (orange) on the surface of a grape vine are seen under a microscope.

Plant Characteristics

Pollen, seeds, and leaves are the most common plant materials recovered. Each species has pollen, seeds, and leaves with different characteristics.

Pollen

Pollen is the fertilising agent produced by the male part of plants, called the anther. It is usually only produced during one or two seasons each year. Pollen comes in an amazing number of sizes and shapes. It can be spiked, pitted, peanut-shaped, round, oblong, and even squarish.

Pollen, as seen by the naked eye

Seeds

Seeds come in an even greater variety of sizes and shapes than pollen. This makes them even easier to tell apart. They may have hooks or barbs, or wings and tails.

Pollen grains, as seen under a microscope

Leaves

There is a great variation in size, shape, structure, and texture between the leaves of different species. They can be hard or soft, thin or thick, smooth or rough, hairless, or covered in fluff or trichomes.

Sunflower seeds, as seen by the naked eye

CASE NOTE

Some seeds have fleshy coverings, such as apples and cherries, that make them attractive to animals. When animals eat the fruits, the seeds are shed in their droppings. Forensic botanists can often identify seeds from animal droppings.

Tiny plant seeds, as seen under a microscope

Wood Characteristics

A plank of wood used as a weapon, a wooden-handled chisel used to break into a house, and the wooden window frames of a house can all produce splinters of wood that can be used as evidence.

Fortunately for forensic botanists, woods differ in color, odor, ring growth patterns, **pores**, and **resin canals**. Processed timbers also differ in their chemical treatments. This makes wood an ideal piece of evidence for investigators to compare and identify.

Under the Microscope

All wood falls into one of two broad groups, hardwoods or softwoods. Despite their name, hardwoods are not necessarily harder than softwoods. These names describe the wood's internal structure.

Hardwoods come from trees other than conifers. Their microscopic structures vary greatly from species to species, but all contain three types of cells, called tracheids, ray cells, and vessels.

bark

heartwood

rings

Cross-section of a tree

Softwoods are the conifer species of trees. They differ from hardwoods because they do not have vessels and 90 to 95 percent of their cells are tracheids.

All trees have up to five layers of wood. Bark is the outermost layer and heartwood is the innermost layer. These layers produce the ring growth on trees, which can also be used for wood identification.

Narcotic and Poisonous Plants

Many plants produce chemicals that are poisonous or narcotic. Narcotics alter the mind to produce one or more of the following feelings or reactions:

- euphoria, which is overwhelming happiness
- hallucinations, which are wild and vivid imaginations
- sedation, which is overwhelming tiredness
- stimulation, which is excessive restlessness and hyperactivity

These reactions are often the cause of fights, violent crimes, crashes, and accidental deaths.

Some narcotic or poisonous plants are illegal to grow, use, or sell. Forensic botanists can be called in to detect whether traces of these plants are present at a scene or to identify plants that are being grown or sold.

Some plants, including narcotic ones, are only poisonous when taken in large quantities. The build-up of the plant chemicals can be toxic or produce an allergic reaction, which can cause bodily organs to shut down. Death can be accidental or intentional.

DID YOU KNOW?

In the past, small doses of marijuana were legally issued by doctors for pain relief.

Marijuana

Angel's trumpet

Magic mushrooms

Poppies

Common Narcotic or Poisonous Plants

These plants are extremely dangerous. Some are especially deadly to small animals and children. They should never be used, even in small quantities.

Marijuana, or cannabis, comes from a plant called *Cannabis sativa*. Its short-term effects include euphoria, relaxation, and loss of concentration. Long-term effects from repeated use include chronic bronchitis, lung cancer, long-term memory loss, and increased risk of mental illness. It is illegal to grow, sell, or use marijuana in most parts of the world.

Angel's trumpet is a widely grown plant with poisonous flowers, leaves, and seeds. When swallowed, it produces side effects such as hallucinations, muscle weakness, increased blood pressure and heart rate, and even paralysis. It can kill small animals and children.

'Magic mushrooms' are mushrooms from the *Psilocybe* group. They are poisonous and bring about hallucinations. Many types of psilocybin mushrooms grow in the wild. It is illegal to pick these wild mushrooms or grow your own.

Poppies are widely grown, but only the species *Papaver somniferum* produces opium. Opium is a sedative used to produce prescription medications such as morphine and codeine. It is illegal to grow opium poppies without a government permit.

Weather, Temperature, and Water

Weather and water can help or hinder forensic investigations. Weather can greatly influence the type of evidence found and how it is interpreted. Water can provide clues as to how and where a person died. It can also destroy or alter evidence.

Weather and Temperature

Air temperature, ground temperature, the season, and the weather can all affect crime evidence or a crime scene. They can affect:

- which insects colonize a corpse
- how quickly insects breed and develop
- how quickly a corpse's body temperature drops
- the time taken for **rigor mortis** to set in
- the time taken for a body to decompose

All these are essential factors in determining the time of death. If a **forensic pathologist** fails to consider the weather and temperature, they could come to the wrong conclusions.

Weather conditions, such as rain and cold temperatures, can affect evidence found at crime scenes.

Water

Water can destroy or alter evidence by:

- washing it away
- causing paper evidence to fall apart or be destroyed
- causing a corpse to bloat and disfigure
- altering how quickly a corpse decomposes

It can mask signs of violence and make time of death estimates inaccurate.

During an autopsy of a person found in water, a pathologist looks for traces of water in the victim's lungs and stomach. When a person drowns, they gulp in water as they struggle to stay afloat. A dead person cannot do this, so finding no water in the victim's lungs or stomach indicates that they were dead before they entered the water.

Sometimes, bodies are swept by currents far away from where they entered the water. Analyzing the water found in the lungs of a washed-up corpse can sometimes help discover where they entered the water. Different water sources have their own mix of salts, chemicals, minerals, plants, and microbes.

Police divers search a river for clues.

The Kidnapping of Charles Lindbergh Jr.

Background

Charles Lindbergh Jr. was the 20-month-old son of Charles and Anne Lindbergh, two of America's most famous pilots. In 1927, Charles Lindbergh Sr. became the first pilot to fly solo, non-stop across the Atlantic Ocean. In 1930, Anne became the first American woman to earn a glider pilot's license.

Bruno Hauptmann was a carpenter from Germany who had been jailed for burglary. He illegally migrated to the United States in 1923.

The crime

On March 1, 1932, Charles Lindbergh Jr. was kidnapped from his family's home and held for ransom. His parents paid the very expensive $50,000 ransom, but Charles was not returned. On May 12, his body was found buried in woods. There was very little useful evidence and the crime remained unsolved for more than two years.

Parts of a hand-made wooden ladder used in the kidnapping of Charles Lindbergh Jr. were found near the Lindberghs' house.

The Evidence

A hand-made wooden ladder was found near the house from which Charles Jr. had been kidnapped. Police asked Dr. Arthur Koehler, an expert in wood anatomy, to examine it. He determined that four types of wood were used to make the ladder. He found marks on some of the wood that allowed him to trace the wood back to the timber yard that processed it.

Dr. Koehler determined that the wood from the top rail of the ladder had probably been cut from a floorboard. He told the police to look for a cut floorboard in their suspect's home.

In September 1934, a man used a gold certificate from the ransom to buy goods in a shop. Gold certificates were an early form of paper money used in the United States. The shop owner wrote the buyer's car license number on the back of the gold certificate. Police traced the license number to a car belonging to Bruno Hauptmann. He was arrested immediately. When police searched his home, they found more gold certificates from the ransom. They also found a floorboard with a piece cut out of it. Dr. Koehler matched the floorboard to the ladder.

Dr. Koehler's evidence was key to the guilty verdict in Hauptmann's 1935 trial. This was the first time botanical evidence was accepted in a U.S. court. Other evidence included the handwritten ransom note, which was matched to samples of Hauptmann's writing.

Bruno Hauptmann was convicted of kidnap and murder.

Investigating the Investigators

Most forensic investigators are police members who have a science, engineering, or other relevant university degree. Outside experts are also involved. The following investigators are just some of the experts involved in investigations that involve bugs, plants, and the environment.

Botanists

Botanists study plants. They can specialize in many fields, such as plant anatomy, biology, or chemistry.

Entomologists

Entomologists study insects. They can specialize in many fields, such as insect anatomy, biology, behavior, or life cycles.

Chemists

Chemists specialize in the various fields of chemistry. They are not pharmacists, who are sometimes also called chemists. Chemists work in many fields in forensic science, from paint analysis to soil analysis.

Geologists

Geologists specialize in the study of the structure and composition of soil and rocks. They often conduct forensic soil analysis.

Forensic Pathologists

Forensic pathologists are medical doctors who specialize in carrying out autopsies. Their main role is to determine how, when, and where a person died, but they also examine wounds on surviving victims. Pathologists often examine bloodstain patterns at the crime scene.

Glossary

botanists	scientists who study plants
compensation	money paid to a victim for any harm or loss they receive at the hands of another person
composition	things something is made up of
contaminants	impurities in something
entomologists	scientists who study insects
erode	wear away
forensic pathologist	medical doctor who specializes in carrying out autopsies
incident	violent, dangerous, or criminal event
infestations	insects present in large numbers, causing damage or disease
macroscopic	visible to the eye without the need for a microscope
mortuaries	places where autopsies are carried out or bodies are stored
narcotics	drugs that are taken to alter the mind rather than for medical purposes
negligence	not taking proper care of something or someone
organic	of living matter
pores	tiny openings in a surface
resin canals	tubes that hold resin, which is the fluid produced by plants to seal up wounds and carry nutrients
rigor mortis	the stiffening of the body shortly after death
silt	type of sand that is carried along by water
sued	brought to court by a person seeking compensation
tread	ridge and groove pattern on tires or the soles of shoes
trichomes	hair-like structures found on plants

Index